THE PIANO MUSIC OF HEITOR VILLA-LOBOS

A New Edition
Revised and Edited by the Composer

Copyright © 1973 by Consolidated Music Publishers
This book published by Amsco Publications,
A Division of Music Sales Corporation, New York, NY.

Order No. AM 41732
International Standard Book Number: 0.8256.4062.8
Library of Congress Catalog Card Number: 73-79787

Exclusive Distributors:
Music Sales Corporation
257 Park Avenue South, New York, NY 10010 USA
Music Sales Limited
8/9 Frith Street, London W1V 5TZ England
Music Sales Pty. Limited
120 Rothschild Street, Rosebery, Sydney, NSW 2018, Australia

Printed in the United States of America by
Vicks Lithograph and Printing Corporation

Amsco Publications
New York • London • Sydney

Dora Alencar de Vasconcellos met Villa-Lobos while serving as the Brazilian Consul-General in New York. During his lifetime, the composer would spend three months of the year in the City and it was during those visits that Madame de Vasconcellos was accorded the rare opportunity of spending every Sunday with the composer and his friends. For her, they were days of extreme pleasure; attending his rehearsals, concerts, and taking part in discussions with the composer and his friends. Thus, Madame de Vasconcellos was in the fortunate position to gather deep insights into the music of her illustrious compatriot.

Madame de Vasconcellos who has been a member of the Brazilian Diplomatic Service for many years is presently her country's Ambassador to Trinidad.
—The Publisher

CONTENTS

FOREWORD

Heitor Villa-Lobos is, undoubtedly, one of the great composers of our time. He was born in Rio de Janeiro, Brazil, in 1887, although the exact year of his birth is still a controversial matter. He died on November 17, 1959. From his earliest age, Villa-Lobos' stern father forced him to participate in concerts of a small chamber orchestra composed of his father and friends and which played in the homes of different members of the ensemble. Even though forced to participate in such concerts, many times even being taken out of bed by his father to do so, Villa-Lobos grew up to be a fierce young composer, unafraid of his beliefs and the mission he knew he had to fulfill, critics notwithstanding. And we should not forget that his musical ideas at the time were simply inconceivable.

He weathered difficult times, playing cello, his favorite instrument, and piano in theaters and movie houses. But in 1922, persons who believed in his musical mission sponsored a trip to Paris. There he was an overnight success. He came under the influence of the Group of Six of France. His success in Paris projected him as a leading composer. His music was different and fascinating: strange and driving rhythms, beautiful and plaintive melodies. The melodies and rhythms sounded strange, for they came from a strange land, Brazil, of which only a few had an idea of what it was. But those Brazilian characteristics were brought to the fore and enhanced by the composer.

Before leaving for Europe, Villa-Lobos had participated in the Movement of Modern Art in Brazil, which marked the introduction of modernism in all forms of art in Brazil. He had been one of the leading exponents of this movement.

With him, the nationalistic expression of art reached its height in Brazil. He was not the one who started the trend, but he was the one responsible for giving it its full meaning.

The moods conveyed in Villa-Lobos's music are tenderness, love, restraint but also passion, intensity and overwhelming inspiration. For it is a soul that communicates with other souls and transmits to them all its joys, anxieties, and intimate emotions. Another very striking feature of Villa-Lobos's music is the sentiment that pervades it. That is the reason why it can be so well understood.

His most striking and original works are the series of BACHIANAS BRA-SILEIRAS and the CHOROS, many of which have been recorded and played in the United States.

I am happy that the publisher had the excellent idea to publish the piano music of Villa-Lobos in one volume. This, I am sure, will give an opportunity for teachers and students to know more about Villa-Lobos and, through his music the culture of Brazil.

—Dora Alencar de Vasconcellos

Authorized Edition

MORENINHA

THE LITTLE PAPER DOLL

No. 2 from
Prolé do Bébé No. 1

H. VILLA-LOBOS
Rio, 1918

Animato molto marcato

Bem cantado

New edition revised by the composer

MULATINHA

THE LITTLE RUBBER DOLL

No. 4 from
Prolé do Bébé No. 1

H. VILLA-LOBOS
Rio, 1918

Un poco animato

Presto

O POLICHINELO

CLOWN
from PROLE DO BÉBÉ No. 1

H. VILLA-LOBOS

Presto

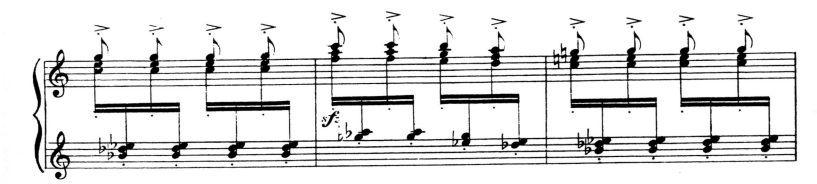

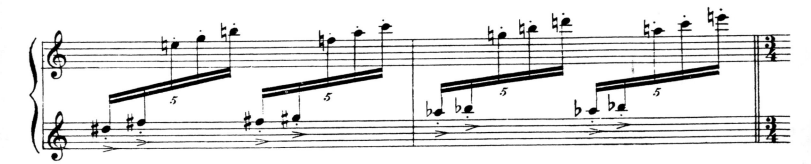

16

il canto distinto

Á Jose Vieira Brandão

1. ACORDEI DE MADRUGADA

DAWN

No. 2 from Album 1
of Guia Prático

H. VILLA-LOBOS
Rio, 1932

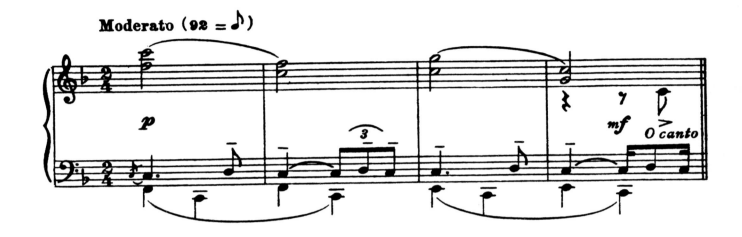

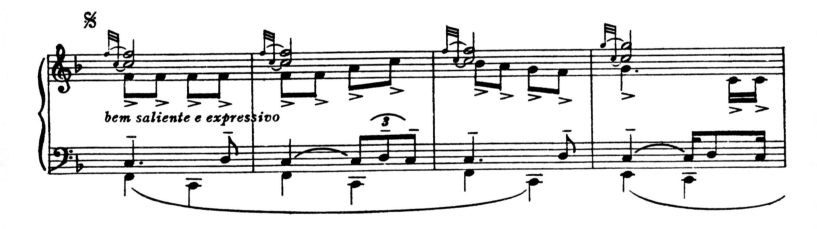

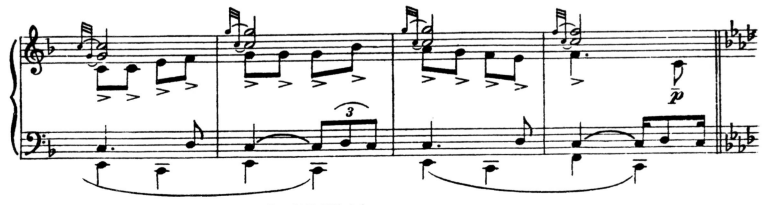

Revised edition by the composer

Á Jose Vieira Brandao

2. A MARE ENCHEU

FULL TIDE

No. 76 from Album 1
of Guia Prático

H. VILLA-LOBOS
Rio, 1932

Revised edition by the composer

Á Jose Vieira Brandao

3. A ROSEIRA

THE ROSE-BUSH

No. 111 from Album 1
of Guia Prático

H. VILLA-LOBOS
Rio, 1932

Revised edition by the composer

Á Jose Vieira Brandao

4. MANQUINHA

LITTLE LAME GIRL

No. 74 from Album 1
of Guia Prático

H. VILLA-LOBOS
Rio, 1932

Á Jose Vieira Brandao

5. NA CORDA DA VIOLA

ON THE STRINGS OF A VIOLA

No. 43 from Album 1
of Guia Prático

H. VILLA-LOBOS
Rio, 1932

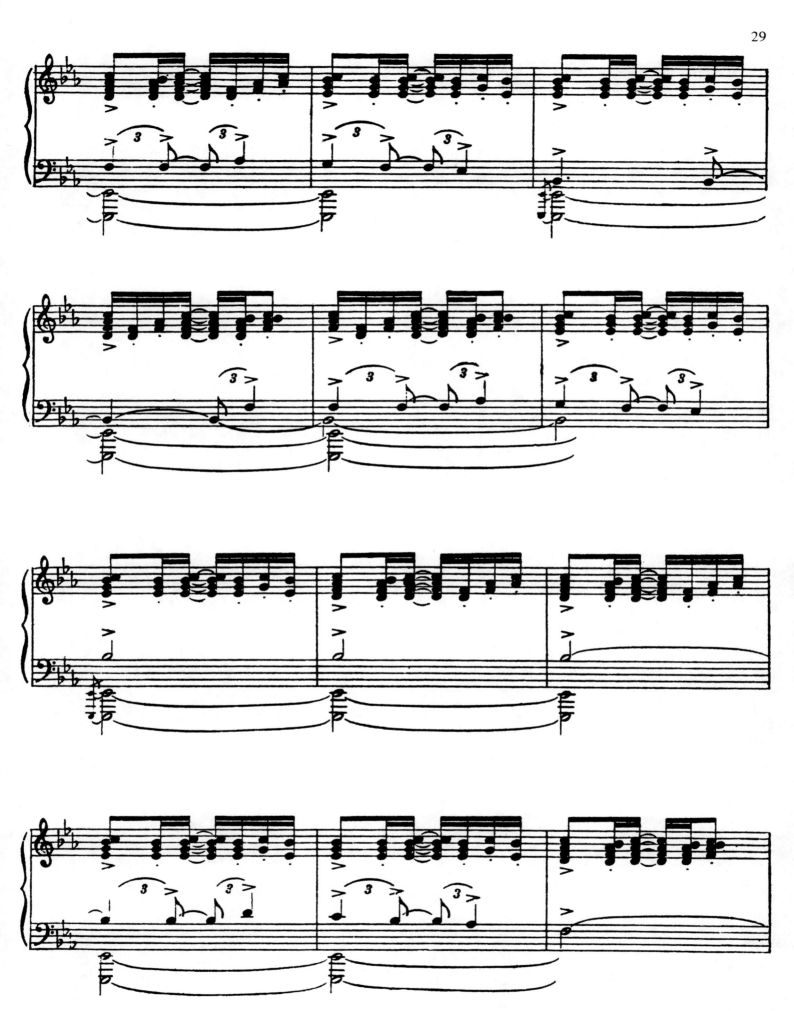

1. O LIMAO

OH, LEMON

No. 68 from Album 8
of Guia Pratico

H. VILLA-LOBOS
Rio, 1935

2. CARAMBOLA

GOODNESS!

No. 28 from Album 8
of Guia Pratico

H. VILLA-LOBOS
Rio, 1935

3. POBRE CEGA

POOR BLIND WOMAN

No. 97 from Album 8
of Guia Pratico

H. VILLA-LOBOS
Rio, 1935

Allegretto moderato ($\quarternote = 63$)

4. PAI FRANCISCO

FATHER FRANCISCO

No. 88 from Album 8
of Guia Pratico

H. VILLA-LOBOS
Rio, 1935

Tempo de Marcha de rancho ($\quad$ = 120)

5. XO! PASSARINHO!

FLY! LITTLE BIRD!

No. 137 from Album 8
of Guia Pratico

H. VILLA-LOBOS
Rio, 1935

Andante (♩ = 56)

6. SINH'ANINHA

FARMERS' DAUGHTERS

No. 120 from Album 8
of Guia Pratico

H. VILLA-LOBOS
Rio, 1935

Andantino (♩ = 104)

7. VESTIDINHO BRANCO

LITTLE WHITE DRESS

No. 131 from Album 8
of Guia Pratico

H. VILLA-LOBOS
Rio, 1935

Molto allegro

1. LARANJEIRA PEQUENINA

THE LITTLE ORANGE TREE

No. 67 from Album 9
of Guia Prático

H. VILLA-LOBOS
Rio, 1935

Allegretto quasi Allegro

2. POMBINHA, ROLINHA

LITTLE DOVE, TINY DOVE

No. 100 from Album 9
of Guia Prático

H. VILLA-LOBOS
Rio, 1935

3. O CIRANDA, O CIRANDINHA

CIRCLE DANCE

No. 35 from Album 9
of Guia Prático

H. VILLA-LOBOS
Rio, 1935

4. A VELHA QUE TINHA NOVE FILHAS

No. 129 from Album 9   THE OLD WOMAN THAT HAD NINE DAUGHTERS

of Guia Prático   **Allegro non troppo**

H. VILLA-LOBOS
Rio, 1935

Em tempo absoluto

5. CONSTANTE

CONSTANT

No. 40 from Album 9
of Guia Prático

H. VILLA-LOBOS
Rio, 1935

Andantino quasi allegretto (M.M. 132 = ♩)

6. O CASTELO

THE CASTLE

No. 32 from Album 9
of Guia Prático

H. VILLA-LOBOS
Rio, 1935

VALSA MISTICA
VALSE MYSTIQUE

No. 1 of Simples Coletanea

H. VILLA-LOBOS
Rio, 1917

EM UM BERÇO ENCANTADO

DANS UN BERCEAU FÉERIQUE

No. 2 of Simples Coletanea

H. VILLA-LOBOS
Rio, 1918

58

(D'après la poésie d'Albert Samain)

RHODANTE

CIRCLE DANCE

No. 3 of Simples Coletanea

H. VILLA-LOBOS
Rio, 1919

64

Á Arnaldo Guinle

ALMA BRASILEIRA

CHOROS No. 5

H. VILLA-LOBOS
Rio, 1925

Lento

A Tomás Terau

PRELUDIO – (Introdução)

PRELUDE - INTRODUCTION

No. 1 from
Bachianas Brasileiras No. 4

H. VILLA-LOBOS
Rio, 1941

New edition revised by the composer

74

A José Vieira Brandão

CORAL – (Canto do Sertão)

CHORAL - SONG OF THE JUNGLE

No. 2 from
Bachianas Brasileiras No. 4

H. VILLA-LOBOS
Rio, 1941

(∗) *Afundar as téclas sem deixar bater os martelos nas cordas.*
Press the keys down without letting hammers strike the strings.

ARIA – (Cantiga)

No. 3 from
Bachianas Brasileiras No. 4

H. VILLA-LOBOS
Rio, 1935

Á Antonietta Rudge

DANSA – (Miudinho)

DANCE

No. 4 from
Bachianas Brasileiras No. 4

H. VILLA-LOBOS
S. Paulo, 1930

À Arminda Neves d'Almeida

PLANTIO DO CABOCLO

NATIVE PLANTING SONG

No. 1 from
Ciclo Brasileiro

H. VILLA-LOBOS
Rio, 1936

Moderato *(em ritmo absoluto)*

New edition revised by the composer

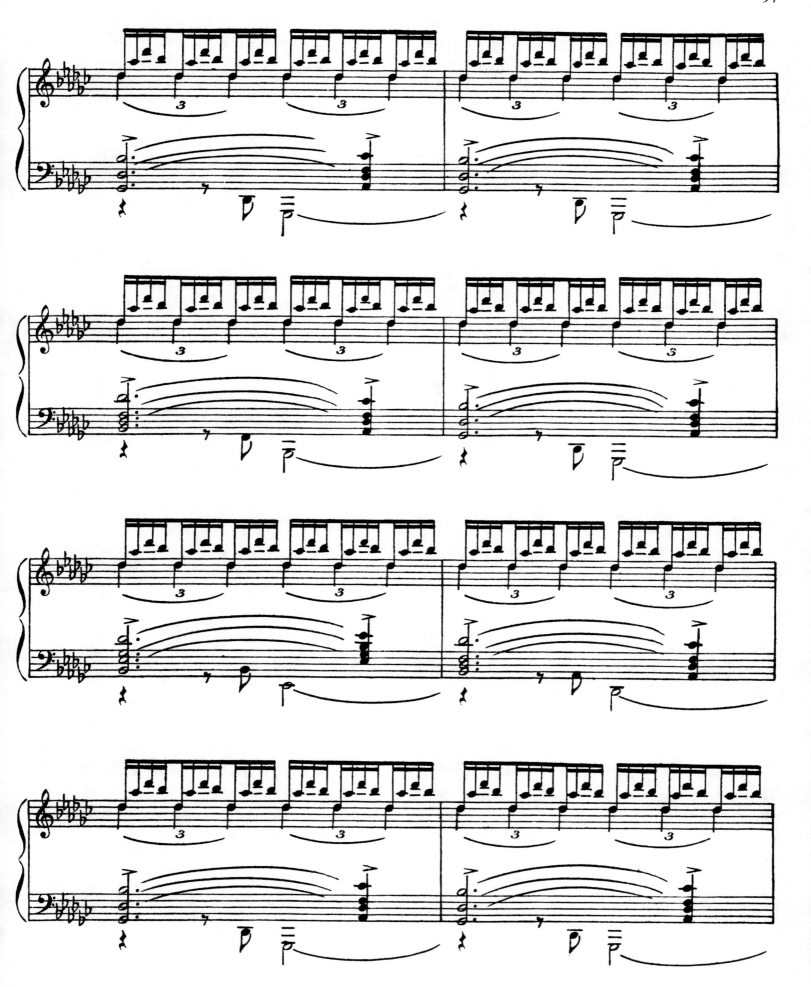

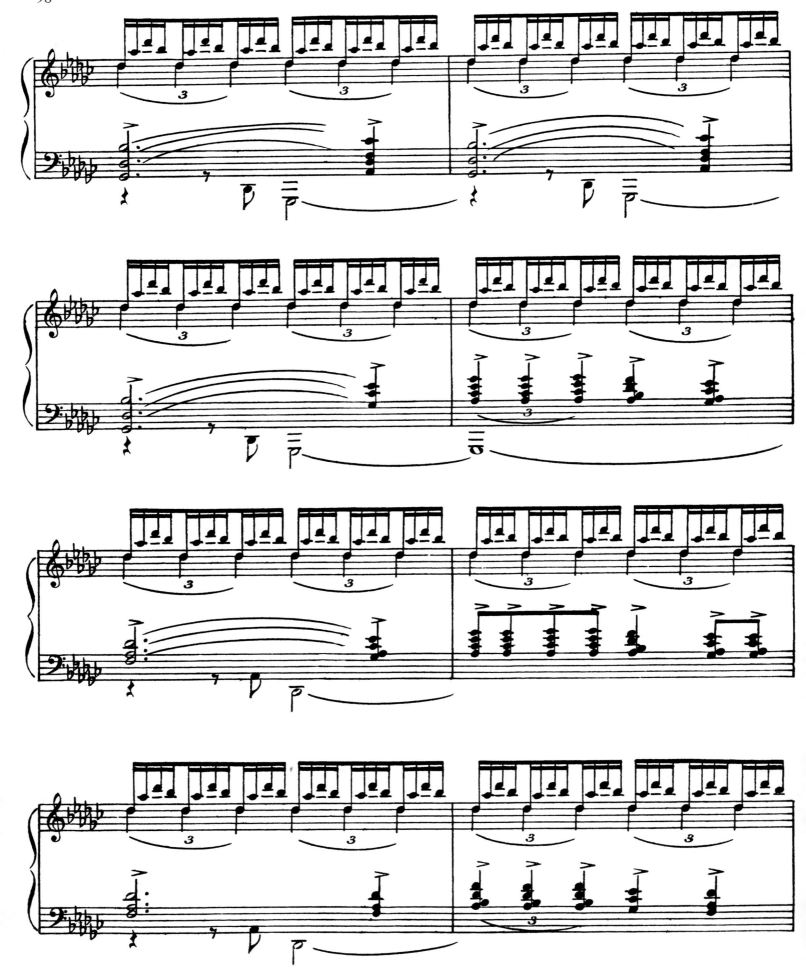

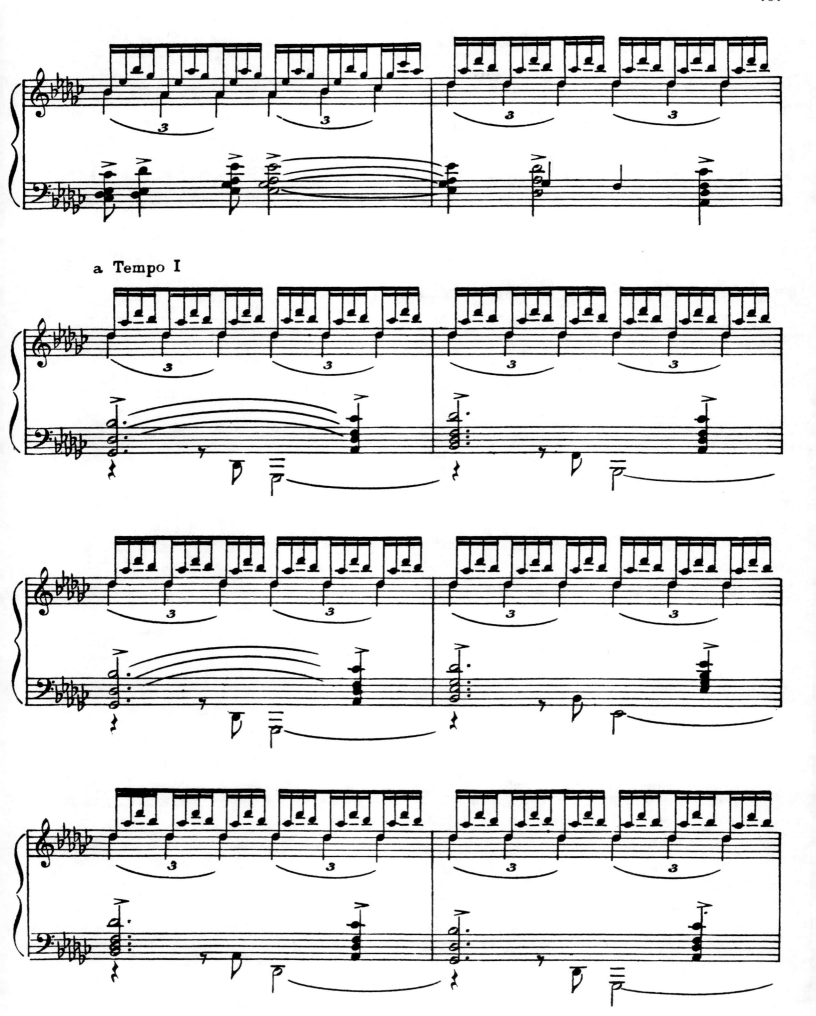

a Tempo I

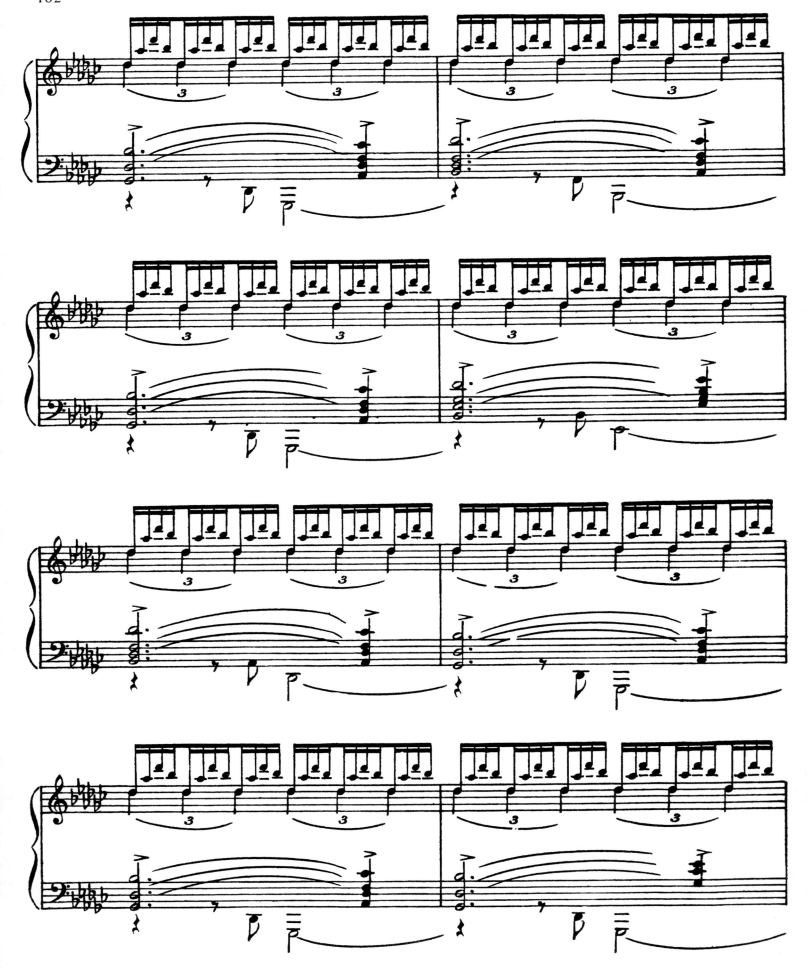

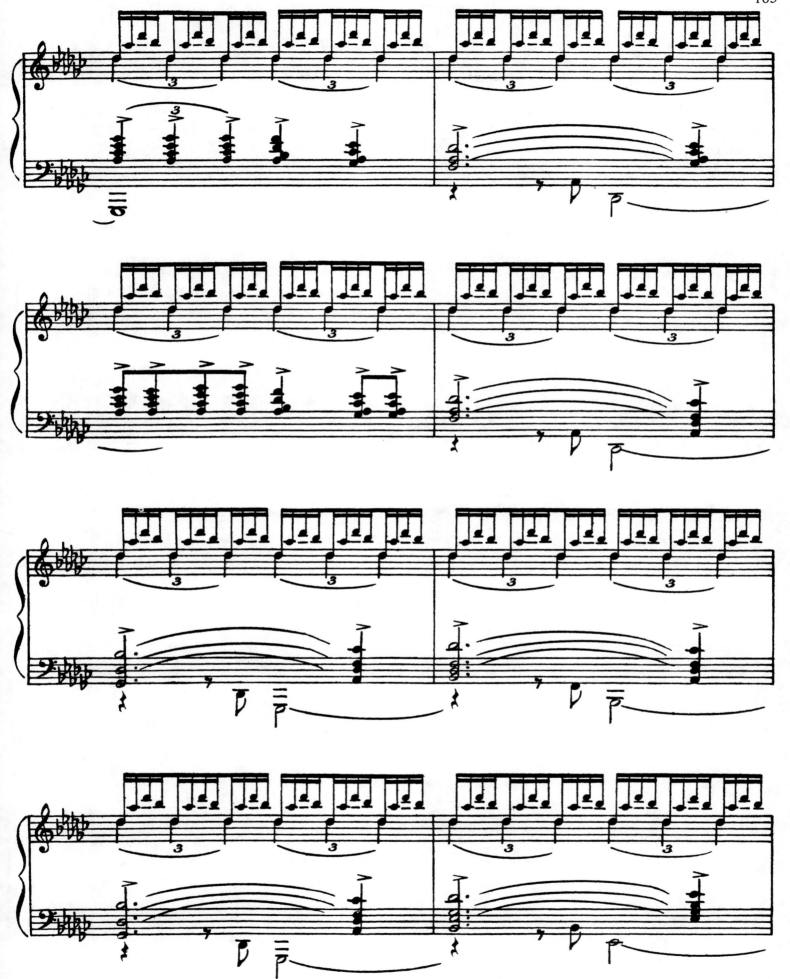

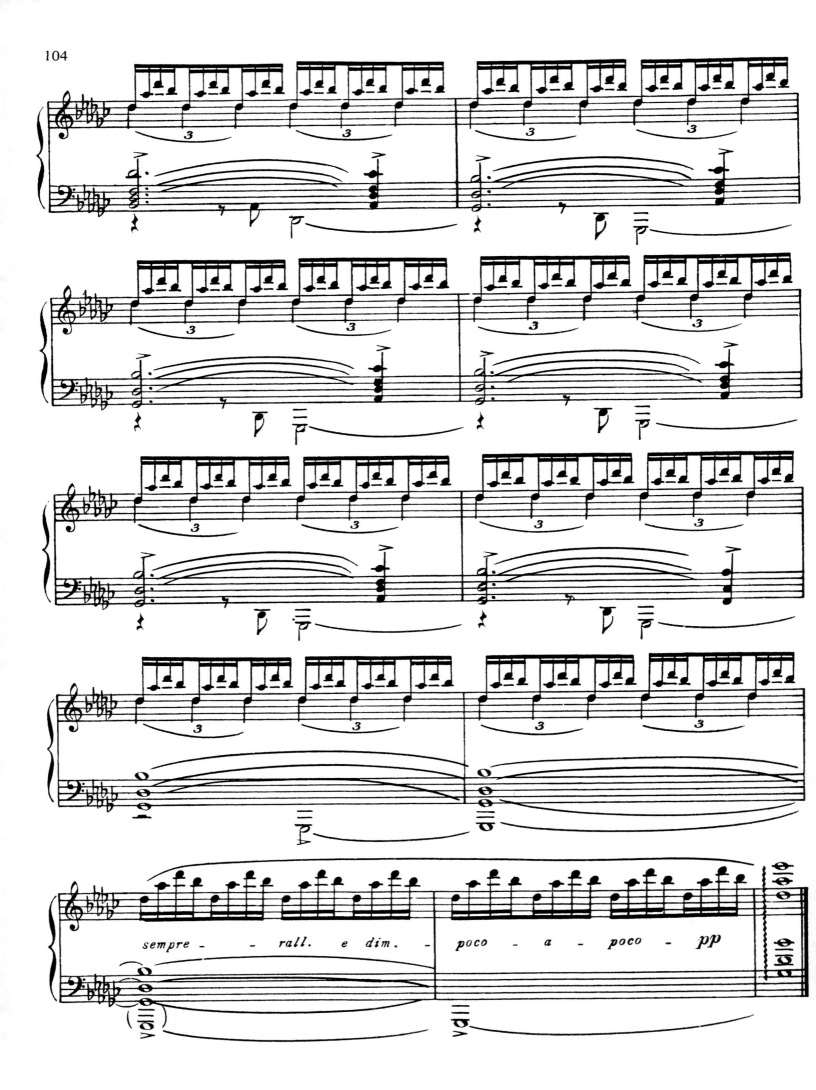

sempre - - rall. e dim. - poco - a - poco - pp

IMPRESSOES SERESTEIRAS

MINSTREL IMPRESSIONS

No. 2 from
Ciclo Brasileiro

H. VILLA-LOBOS
Rio, 1936

Più mosso (*Allegro*)

Moderato

Animato

A Arminda Neves d'Almeida

FESTA NO SERTAO

JUNGLE FESTIVAL

No. 3 from
Ciclo Brasileiro

H. VILLA-LOBOS
Rio, 1937

Allegro animato

Tempo I°

123

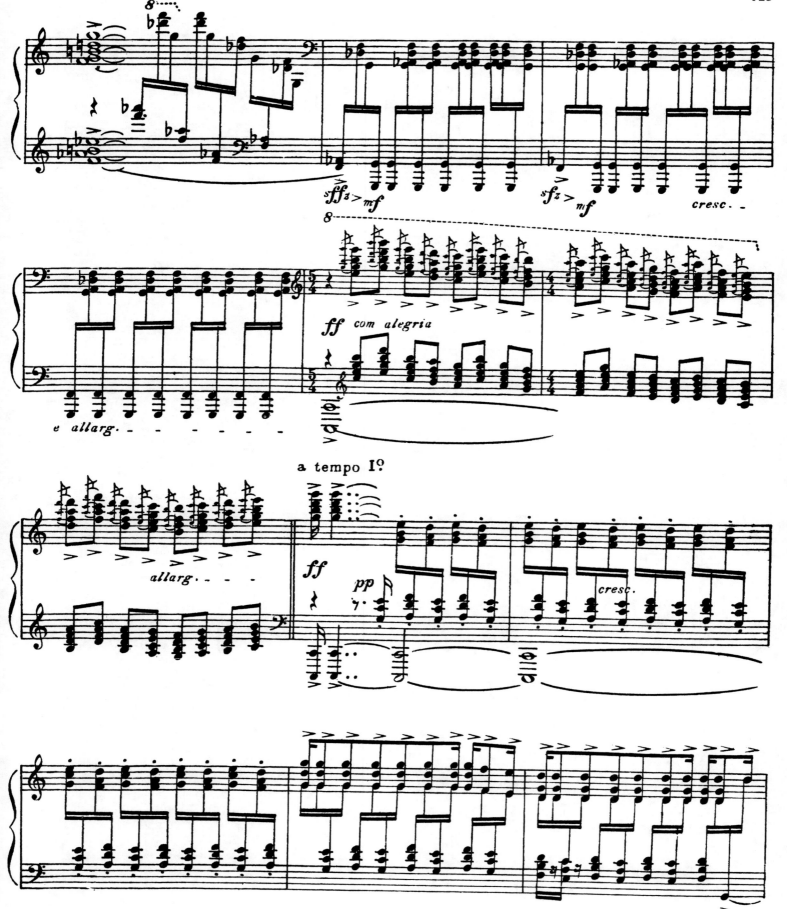

125

Molto animato

A Arminda Neves d'Almeida

DANSA DO INDIO BRANCO

DANCE OF THE WHITE INDIAN

No. 4 from
Ciclo Brasileiro

H. VILLA-LOBOS
Rio, 1936

ALLEGRO

New edition revised by the composer

Muito cantada

Sem sair da uniformidade absoluta do ritmo

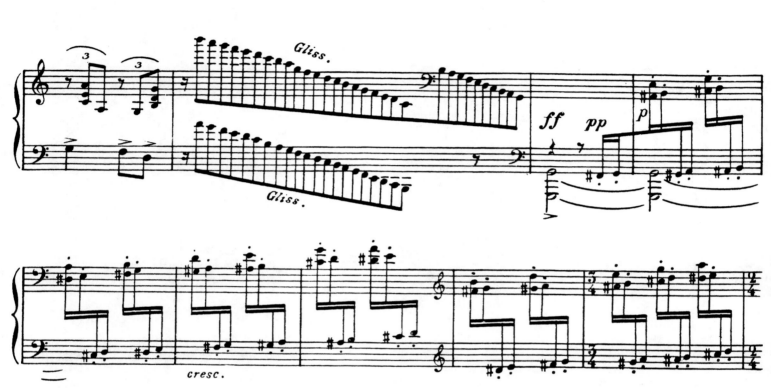

IDILIO NA REDE

SUMMER IDYLL

No. 1 from
Suite Floral

H. VILLA-LOBOS
Rio, 1917

Acalanto (♩.=98)

UMA CAMPONEZA CANTADEIRA
A SINGING COUNTRY GIRL

No. 2 from
Suite Floral

H. VILLA-LOBOS
Rio, 1916

ALEGRIA NA HORTA

JOY IN THE GARDEN
(Impressions of a festival of gardeners)

No. 3 from
Suite Floral

H. VILLA-LOBOS
Rio, 1918

POUCO ANIMADO

Revised edition by the composer

Authorized Edition

A MANHA DA PIERRETE

PIERRETTE'S HANDS

No. 3 from
Carnaval das Criancas

H. VILLA-LOBOS
Rio, 1919

Allegretto capriccietto

New edition revised by the composer

Authorized Edition

O CHICOTE DO DIABINHO

THE DEVIL'S WHIP

No. 2 from
Carnaval das Criancas Brasileiras

H. VILLA-LOBOS
Rio, 1919

CAIXINHA DE MUSICA QUEBRADA
THE BROKEN LITTLE MUSIC BOX

H. VILLA-LOBOS
S. Paulo, 1931

Pouco animado.

A Arminda Neves d'Almeida

POEMA SINGELO

SIMPLE SONG

H. VILLA-LOBOS
Rio, 1942

Andantino

8ª abaixo

8ª abaixo

8ª abaixo

164

166